GREEK ISLANDS

Life most beautiful

GREEK ISLANDS

Life most beautiful

HERRON

THE GREEK ISLANDS

'It takes a lifetime to discover Greece,
but it only takes an instant to fall in love with her.'

— HENRY MILLER

Greek island life: sun-kissed, soul-deep. The Aegean serves it all in bold, intoxicating doses.

Blue-domed churches reaching up to meet the sky, cobbled streets bursting with bougainvillea, olive groves as far as the eye can see. Superyachts parked like trophies, private villas with infinity pools, clifftop tavernas where the scent of grilled octopus drifts on the breeze. It's all so picture-perfect, you might wonder if it's real.

Almost part of the national identity, the Cyclades are Greece's stars. And if Mykonos and Santorini are the celebrity headliners —the Beyoncé and Jay-Z, drawing every camera and crowd—then Paros and Antiparos are their effortlessly cool indie counterparts; think Florence Pugh and Timothée Chalamet: chic, low-key and completely in-the-know without trying. They're where you go to skip the velvet rope and the throngs of fans but still get that Aegean allure and boho style.

The Ionian Islands? They bring a touch of Italian flair to the Greek spirit. Corfu is the queen of this lush chain, all Venetian mansions, elegant squares and artfully crumbling villas.

For something more off-radar, Homer's legendary island, Ithaca, is a peaceful, lesser-known beauty where you can slip into a crystal-clear bay and feel like you've travelled back centuries.

For a taste of old-world Greece, the Saronic Islands are just a hop, skip and jump from Athens. Hydra, car-free and bohemian, is an artist's dream; while Spetses—the sophisticated sibling—mixes maritime history with boutique hotels and seafront dining fit for a James Bond film.

In the Dodecanese, Rhodes stands as the bold classic, with medieval walls and ancient ruins drawing admirers year-round. But Symi quietly dazzles with pastel houses cascading down the hillsides. Understated, photogenic and unpolished, Symi has that 'if you know, you know' magic.

With 6,000 islands and islets, only 227 inhabited, the Greek Islands are a world of their own. Whether you're craving glitz, glamour or simply a seat at the local taverna, the Greek Islands are ready to serve it up to you in style.

THE CYCLADES

SANTORINI

RESTAURANT

OIA, SANTORINI

A cliché? Maybe. But this Cycladic hotspot flaunts its blue-domed churches and sunset views like a seasoned pro, creating a vibe that even the most jaded traveller won't be able to resist. Sure, it's on every bucket list, but some places are just that good—and Oia is one of them.

Beyond those iconic views, local artists, boutique designers and cosy tavernas remind you that Oia's charm goes deeper than the postcard shot. As the sun dips behind the caldera, the energy shifts. Find your rooftop perch, forget the Insta-crowds and just lean into the magic.

AMORGOS

NAXOS

MYKONOS

PARTY SPOTS

'The early bird catches the worm, but the late bird gets a longer siesta.'

— UNKNOWN

The Greek Islands know how to throw a party, and nowhere does it better than Mykonos. Flaunting its reputation as the 'Ibiza of Greece', this island has perfected the art of beachside glamour, where top-tier beach clubs draw a crowd of models, moguls and those just looking to sip designer cocktails with their toes in the sand. At Nammos, expect DJs spinning into the sunset, exclusive cabanas and a world-class menu—all set against the glistening Aegean. Scorpios is more bohemian chic, with its earthy decor and sprawling terraces that feel like an ancient amphitheatre reimagined for the jet set. Sunsets here are a ritual, with beats filling the air as day fades into night.

For a more laid-back scene, the island of Paros is stepping up with its own brand of beachside cool. The club scene on Santa Maria Beach is catching on fast, with DJs and cocktails cultivating a vibrant yet unpretentious vibe. For a chic night out, the clubs in Naoussa are for stylish locals and in-the-know travellers mingling in the narrow, bar-lined alleys, dancing till dawn.

Then there's Ios, the Aegean's unfiltered party island, with Mylopotas Beach at its core. The legendary FarOut Beach Club keeps the energy alive with pool parties, big-name DJs and a buzzing crowd. Days blur into nights here, where beach lounging effortlessly transitions into high-energy parties under the stars. Expect neon-lit nights, late-morning swims and a carefree vibe that captures the island's hedonistic spirit. This is where you'll find the island's younger, edgier crowd letting loose, with no plans of calling it a night anytime soon.

MYKONOS

Once a beloved party spot for the gay community, Mykonos doesn't just attract a crowd—it commands one. It's unapologetic, glamorous and undeniably unforgettable, with gleaming white alleys twisting like a labyrinth and chic boutiques spilling style onto the cobblestones.

Little Venice is a sunset dream, where you'll find the beautiful, the bold and the fabulously famous sipping cocktails as the light fades. By night, head to the beach clubs where sun-kissed dancers move under starlit skies as world-class DJs set the soundtrack for an unforgettable night on the Aegean.

SERIFOS

UP-AND-COMING ISLANDS

'The isles of Greece, the isles of Greece! Where burning Sappho loved and sung, where grew the arts of war and peace, where Delos rose, and Phoebus sprung!'

— LORD BYRON

Sure, Santorini and Mykonos steal the spotlight with their blue domes and superyachts, but beyond the classics there's a whole spectrum of spots where you can escape the sunset-snapping crowds. These islands are redefining the Greek getaway—a siren's call for those who know there's more to paradise than the obvious.

Fast becoming the Cycladic island on everyone's lips, Milos still has that slightly rough-around-the-edges vibe that savvy travellers covet. Wind-sculpted, lunar-white cliffs plunge into emerald waters and sweet boathouses are dotted along the shore like a painter's palette. The sea caves—once pirate hideouts—are only reachable by boat, adding a dash of intrigue to the thrill of discovery. If you're craving something fresh, something real, Milos serves it up in spades.

Then there's Antiparos—Paros' effortlessly cool neighbour that's all about low-key luxury. Here, you won't find Mykonos glitz; instead, you'll be sipping strong cocktails in low-key tavernas and sunbaking on secluded beaches. Antiparos Town has a laid-back, artsy spirit, while just off the coast, untouched Despotiko will tempt travellers seeking serious bragging rights.

Folegandros? Pure drama, with sunsets that rival the best of Santorini without the fuss. The village of Chora, perched high above the sea, will captivate with whitewashed houses and views that stretch endlessly into the blue. If you want a slice of authentic Greece with a side of jaw-dropping scenery, this one's perfect for you.

Last, but definitely not least, is Kythira, tucked away from the tourist trail and all the better for it. It's not easy to reach, but once you're here you'll be drawn in, hook, line and sinker. This is an island that keeps its secrets close, in its rolling hills, Venetian castles, hidden waterfalls and deserted beaches. The pace here is so gentle you can't help but fall into step.

ANTIPAROS

SIFNOS

SIFNOS

Known for its sizzling food scene, this tiny island has become a magnet for those who appreciate the art of slow living and exceptional cuisine.

In Apollonia, the scent of roasting lamb and dill wafts through the air, while sweet Artemonas offers stunning whitewashed lanes that lead to family-run bakeries and tavernas serving up creamy *revithada* and delicate almond biscuits.

End your day at a cliffop wine bar, savouring sunset views over a glass of Assyrtiko. Life here is as delicious and unhurried as it gets.

FAROS

MOST INSTAGRAMMABLE VIEWS

'The problem with Greece is that she's just too beautiful.'

— UNKNOWN

The Greek Islands are #instagoals, every time. Around every corner is a shot just waiting for that perfect filter—think sun-bleached beaches, cliffside tavernas and alleyways dripping with bougainvillea. There's probably even a cat lounging like a true influencer. But a few spots? They're basically made for your feed.

The queen of Insta has to be Santorini. If you haven't snapped Oia's famous blue domes against a blazing sunset, did you even go to Greece? The caldera view, with whitewashed houses spilling down the cliffs, is like an artwork come alive. Come dusk, the sky turns a hazy lavender, and suddenly it's #nofilternecessary. Bonus points if you're perched on a rooftop with a cocktail in hand, literally living your best life.

Then there's Mykonos. Its Little Venice is pure magic—whitewashed buildings hovering over the water, vibrant balconies popping with colour and those iconic windmills perfectly positioned to catch the last rays of the day. This spot wasn't just made for golden hour; it defines it. And Scorpios? It's the beach club that dreams are made of, with bronzed bodies lounging on daybeds, to-die-for views and that just-right lighting. Snap a pic and watch the likes roll in.

For something less expected but equally jaw-dropping, Milos has you covered. Sarakiniko Beach's surreal white cliffs and crystal-clear waters have lunar vibes straight out of a sci-fi movie. The place is a blank canvas for photos—and trust us, your grid will thank you.

Over in the Ionian Islands, Zakynthos' Shipwreck Beach is epic, with an old rusted shipwreck on perfect white sand, framed by dramatic cliffs and ridiculously blue water. Find the lookout point above for the ultimate bucket-list shot.

Finally, Hydra is the island if you like it low-key and artsy. With car-free streets, stone mansions and a harbour full of fishing boats, it's like a step back in time—and your followers will totally feel it.

MILOS

MILOS

This is becoming Greeece's hottest island to watch, a honeypot of a Cycladic escape that's luring attention away from Mykonos and Santorini with its ethereal landscapes and quieter feel. Sarakiniko's lunar-like white cliffs and Kleftko's sea caves with striking turquoise pools are an oh-so-fresh take on the very concept of an island paradise. Beyond Milos' photogenic beaches, chic seaside cafes and boutique hotels blend Cycladic style with laid-back luxury. It's undeniably authentic and quintessentially Greek. What more could you possibly want?

THE IONIAN ISLANDS

KEFALONIA

CORFU

ISLAND FLAVOURS

'Greek food is not about complexity, but about a perfect balance of ingredients.'

— DIANE KOCHILAS

Each island has its own flavour-packed dishes; sun-drenched, sea-salted and steeped in tradition. You'll find common threads, sure: fresh herbs, robust olive oil, creamy cheeses and a devotion to ingredients. But geography, climate and centuries of trade and conquest have uniquely shaped the flavours. The influences of Venetians, Ottomans and North African traders ripple through recipes, resulting in a cuisine that's both quintessentially Greek yet distinct to each isle.

In Kefalonia, seafood takes centre stage. Here, feast on grilled octopus, tender and smoky; or mussels in saffron-spiked broth, best enjoyed with a view over the Ionian Sea. Nearby, Zakynthos magics up grilled-to-perfection squid stuffed with local cheese and herbs, a perfect snapshot of Ionian flavours.

It's all about the land on Naxos—think slow-roasted lamb, tangy local cheeses and potatoes so famous they've become an island trademark. This is Greek food at its most elemental, rooted in simplicity but bursting with flavour. And if it's carbs you crave, Ikaria—known for its long-living locals—delivers with handmade pasta enriched with goat's milk and wild herbs, a dish that feels like (and probably is) a culinary secret passed down through generations of wrinkled grandmothers.

The kitchen is almost sacred on Sifnos, with chickpea stews and almond cakes that bring warmth to every table. In Santorini, try white eggplant and fava beans grown in volcanic soil, imparting an intense, unique flavour that's unlike anything else.

And Crete's flavours are bold and unforgettable. Here, rich, earthy olive oil—some of the finest in the world—is drizzled over everything, from fresh vegetables to slow-cooked meats. And there's the honey, amber, aromatic and renowned for its health benefits, slathered over yogurt or baked into pastries that taste like sunshine.

This is the kind of food that calls to you when you're back home on a rainy day—food that feeds your imagination, yet somehow never quite tastes the same when you try to recreate it.

CORFU TOWN

If Corfu is the star of the Ionian Islands, all timeless glamour and effortless charisma, then its eponymous main town is a scene-stealer in its own right. Beguiling, storied and elegant, you'll find Venetian mansions, cafés pouring icy frappés and the grand Liston promenade where locals stroll like it's a daily runway.

The hum of life here blends Greek soul with a touch of Venetian, French and British flair, and the result is sun-drenched, timeless and effortlessly chic—Corfu's very own take on *la dolce vita*. Sip a spritz at a tucked-away wine bar, and you'll see what we mean.

LEFKADA

ZAKYNTHOS

THE SARONIC ISLANDS

HYDRA

Hydra isn't here to dazzle; it's here to cast a quieter spell. A hop, skip and a jump from Athens, the stunning car-free island swaps engines for donkey hooves and whitewashed houses for stone mansions, legacies of its wealthy maritime past.

In the harbour, fishing boats bob alongside chic yachts while the air carries hints of sea salt and grilled octopus from low-key tavernas. It's the unpolished details that make Hydra a standout: artisan workshops hidden behind ivy-covered doors; the soft clang of church bells drifting down from the hills.

THE DODECANESE

RHODES

Rhodes has always been a prize worth fighting for: once a sun-soaked stepping stone for traders and crusaders, today it's one of Greece's most beloved holiday escapes.

Rhodes Town is all stone arches and maze-like lanes wrapped in medieval walls; Lindos dazzles with its ancient acropolis perched above turquoise bays; and villages such as Apollona keep age-old crafts alive. Explore pine-covered mountains spilling into beach resorts, sip sunset cocktails in Mandraki Harbour and lose yourself in the ancient ruins of Kamiros, where history comes alive under the Aegean sun.

SYMI

SYMI

Little Symi is big on charm and colour. As you sail into the prettiest port in Greece, pastel-hued mansions rise like a dream out of the sea. Don't be daunted by the 500 steps up to the acropolis; up here, the pace slows and the views amaze. Back down, among the well-heeled yachties and curious day-trippers from Rhodes, you'll lean into a sophisticated simplicity: watch fishermen mending nets by the harbour, sip ouzo at a waterfront *kafeneio* or browse for handmade ceramics in tiny artisan shops. It's an island where the small pleasures linger long after you leave.

IKARIA

WELLNESS ESCAPES

'In all things of nature there is something of the marvellous.'

— ARISTOTLE

Looking to reset and recharge? The Greek Islands are upping the game with a wave of upmarket retreats where infinity pools and holistic therapies meet Cycladic sunsets and organic Greek produce. Think deep-tissue massages with olive oil, private yoga sessions on secluded beaches and treatments infused with local herbs.

But beyond these luxury spas and boutique retreats, Greece's wellness scene has been thriving for centuries. On the islands, you'll find timeless treatments in wild settings taking centre stage.

Ikaria is the original slow-living poster child. It's one of the world's Blue Zones, where locals famously live long and well. The secret might be in the simplicity—and the thermal springs that have bubbled up along the coast since ancient times. The mineral-rich waters, nestled among rugged cliffs and olive groves, are said to alleviate arthritis, stress and even skin ailments. Slip into the warmth and let the island's unhurried pace melt your worries away.

Kos has been synonymous with wellness since the days of Hippocrates. The Agios Fokas thermal springs, where volcanic-heated waters meet the Aegean, create a natural hot-tub experience that feels like a prescription for the soul. The setting is dramatic: rock pools with emerald waters that shimmer under the sunlight, and the distant scent of salty air mixed with volcanic steam.

Over on Milos, luxury comes in a different form—straight from the earth. The mud baths at Aliki offer a DIY spa experience where you slather on nutrient-rich volcanic mud and let it bake under the sun's heat. The results? Silky-smooth skin and a glow that no high-end spa treatment can replicate.

And for something more exclusive, head to Santorini's Palea Kameni. This volcanic island, accessible only by boat, hides sulphur-rich hot springs that bubble up in shades of gold and are famous for their skin-softening properties. Floating here, surrounded by the caldera's sheer cliffs, is a wellness experience as dramatic as it is restorative.

PATMOS

CHORA, PATMOS

This vision of whitewashed alleys, bougainvillea-draped walls and centuries-old mansions, all clustered around the mighty Monastery of St John, is so beautiful it's no wonder UNESCO gave it World Heritage status.

Patmos is a holy island, and there's a palpable spiritual vibe in the air. Vaulted passageways lead past Byzantine chapels while stone steps twist towards surprising sea views. Slip into an unmarked doorway for honey-drenched pitas from a family-run bakery, or sip chilled ouzo at Yorgos' tiny *kafeneio*, where locals share stories.

MEDITERRANEAN VIBES

'Greek architecture is the flowering of geometry.'

— RALPH WALDO EMERSON

The sensuous curves of Cycladic architecture are unmistakable: white buildings with thick walls to ward off the midday heat, and domes that echo the Aegean's blue. But look closer, and you'll see stories in every detail—cobalt shutters framing the sea and aged doors that have weathered decades of salt-laden breezes.

Elsewhere, islands like Hydra and Symi bring a different aesthetic. Hydra's cobbled, car-free lanes lead you past stone mansions with rustic wooden doors and grand arches, while Symi's pastel-hued harbour and bougainvillea-draped balconies add a splash of Italian flair to its Greek elegance. Both islands bring their own interpretation of Mediterranean beauty, but share a laid-back pace and a deep connection to the sea and sky.

In the northeast, the Dodecanese Islands blend Byzantine fortresses and medieval splendour. Patmos, with its whitewashed chapels and serene atmosphere, feels almost monastic; while Rhodes dazzles with its Old Town—cobbled streets and towering stone walls that transport you to the era of the Crusades.

Together, the islands form a mosaic of Mediterranean elegance, where every structure and pathway celebrates natural beauty.

Inside is no different, where the Greek Islands have style down to an art. Interiors are all about texture and simplicity. Stone floors meet woven rugs, hand-carved stools sit by low tables, terracotta pots hold sprigs of rosemary and mint, and linens gently catch the breeze. It's all about minimalist design in earthy tones and open spaces that invite nature in.

Outside, terraces look out over endless blue, shaded by pergolas dressed in vines. Picture a long table set for lunch, a cloth billowing in the breeze, surrounded by olive trees and pops of pink bougainvillea. Sun-soaked by day and candle-lit by night, these terraces are the heart of island life, one that's relaxed, unhurried and deeply in tune with the rhythms of nature.

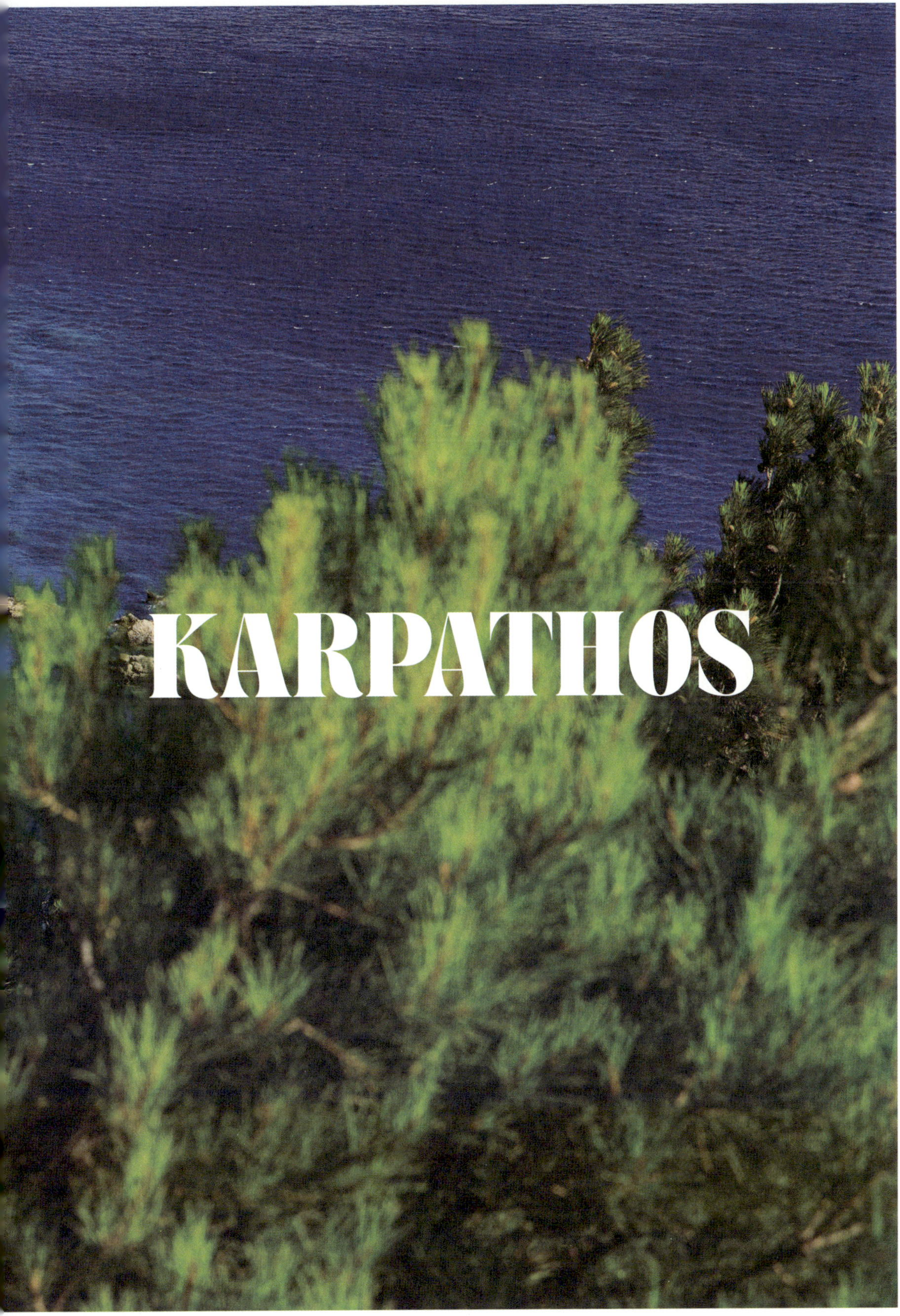
KARPATHOS

CRETE

CRETE

You might come to the world's 88th largest island for the beaches. But you'll likely stay for the onion-peel layers of intrigue that make it so much more than a sun-soaked getaway. Centuries of life overlap here: ancient cities like Heraklion and Chania; Byzantine monasteries perched in the hills; and a rich tapestry of civilisations—from the Minoans to the Venetians and Ottomans—woven into every corner. Marvel at the storied Palace of Knossos, trek through the dramatic gorges and sip raki in tucked-away mountain villages where it feels like time never moved on.

First Published in 2025 by Herron Book Distributors Pty Ltd
14 Manton St
Morningside
QLD 4170
www.herronbooks.com

Custom book production by Captain Honey Pty Ltd
12 Station Street
Bangalow
NSW 2479
www.captainhoney.com.au

Front cover image by Michela Ravasio © Stocksy.com
Cover and internal design by Natalie Winter
Image selection by Natalie Winter
Images © Shutterstock.com
Words by Ellie Cobb

Cataloguing-in-Publication. A catalogue record for this book is available from the National Library of Australia

ISBN 978-1-923279-45-2

Printed and bound in China

5 4 3 2 1 25 26 27 28 29